Animal
Love

Love is a four-legged word.

When I needed a hand,
I found your paw.

Behind every great person, there is a great animal.

**Stand tall and never be afraid
to show your true colors.**

Sunshine doesn't come from the sky, it comes from the love of animals.

Animals are a gift.

Life is better with fish.

All you need is love and animals.

An animal's eyes speak a powerful language.

Take time to breathe in the fresh air.

**All good things are wild
and free.**

A little love makes
a big difference.

Enjoy the ride along the way.

The road to my heart is paved
with paw prints.

It's better to be wild
than boring.

**The best therapy for your soul
has fur and soft ears.**

Wild birds fly free.

Be like a fish and
go with the flow.

Wild hearts can't be broken.

We need animals as much as they need us.

Animals make our lives whole.

Animal love is the best love.

**Birds will always sing a song
for those who will listen.**

Time spent with an animal is never wasted.

**Animals may not speak,
but they do know how to listen.**

Animals show us how powerful unconditional love can be.

**The sea is full of beauty
and wonder.**

Some angels choose fur instead of wings.

If animals could talk,
they wouldn't.

Some things fill your heart without even trying.

Life is warmer with an animal by your side.

**People who help animals have
the biggest hearts.**

Happiness is having an animal as a friend.

Take care of an animal and it will love you forever.

Home is where your dog is.

**Be kind to every kind,
not just mankind.**

There is no better explorer than a bird.

**A great rider can hear
his horse whisper.**